The Blue Eye

Rescue!

Dutch Adventure

The Finest in the Land

The Flying Machine

Key Trouble

Introduction

The stories in Stage 9 More Stories A continue the aims begun in Stage 8 in helping to develop confident independent readers, and preparing them for conventional text layouts.

The longer books at Stage 9 require greater reading stamina and an appreciation of more complex plots. Although the language is still controlled, sentences are longer, more complex, and start with a wider range of openings.

It remains important to introduce the story through discussion, not only to enable children to read with confidence, but also to foster prediction skills.

Vocabulary includes a high proportion of the NLS high frequency word lists and children are encouraged to use their phonemic knowledge and other strategies to deal with the wider vocabulary. The plots encourage children to empathise and become aware of other viewpoints and they engender an understanding of a wider range of stories.

How to introduce the books

At Stage 9 it is still important for children to talk about the story before beginning to read aloud: longer sentences mean that children need to carry the sense of the unfolding story in their heads for longer and story lines are more complex, involving sub plots within each story. In addition, the type of story needs discussion.

Before reading, talk about the cover and title, including information about the author, illustrator, the kind of story it might be, and the design features.

Go through the book, looking at the pictures and using or pointing out words which might prove difficult. Ask leading questions so that children will have a context when they come to read. Encourage the use of strategies such as using illustrations, as well as syntactic, semantic and phonic knowledge.

This booklet provides suggestions for using the books in group and independent reading activities. Prompts and ideas are provided for introducing and reading each book with a child or group of children. Suggestions are also provided for writing, speaking and listening activities, and cross-curricular links. You can use these suggestions to follow on from your reading or use at another time.

Take-Home Cards are also available for each book. These provide friendly prompts and suggestions for parents reading with their children. You can store the relevant card with each book in your "Take-Home" selection of titles.

Reading skills

Stage 9 develops:
- confident, independent reading
- awareness of more complex sentences
- understanding of a wider range of stories, beyond everyday experience
- awareness of more complex plots
- a readiness for conventional text layout
- inferential comprehension skills
- awareness of other viewpoints
- insights into feelings and motives of characters
- consolidation of independent writing skills.

Vocabulary chart

The Blue Eye	**Year 2 High frequency words** after again an as back but called came can't could do don't door down first had help her here him house if jump(ed) just little man many much must not off old one out over people pull put ran seen some that them there these took very were what where who with your
	Context words aeroplane alleys arranged awning brought charmer chasing collection covered dangerous engine glowed kingdom marbles motorbike narrow package Princess spilled sprinted stalls thought tilted trapped upstairs
Rescue!	**Year 2 High frequency words** after again an another as back be been but called came can't could did do don't door(s) down first from got had has have help her here his home how if just last laugh(ed) made make many more next not now off one out over people push(ed) put ran saw some take that their them then there these time too us very want water were what where will would your
	Context words aeroplane boulder bubbles circle distance edge goggles gorge jolted kidnapped managed mountains narrow noise palace pilot remembered tightly tubes tyres waste wrecked

Vocabulary chart

Dutch Adventure	**Year 2 High frequency words**
	about after again an as back boy but by called came can't could did down from girl got had have help her here him his home house how jump just laugh(ed) made man more must name not now old one out over people push pull(ed) put ran should so some take that their them then there these time two us very want water way were what where will would(n't)
	Context words
	bicycle cereal cheese diamonds driving dyke Edam fence flood half heavy Holland Mayor pour reward specials squashed stolen taste thief villagers worried
The Finest in the Land	**Year 2 High frequency words**
	about after again an another as back be been boy(s) but by called came can't could did do don't from girl good got had has have help her here him his home how just last love made man many must next not now off one our out people put ran saw should so some that them then there three time too two us very want way were what when who will with would your
	Context words
	castle daughter dungeons entertainers guitar horse instruments juggler kazoo married mixture musicians practicing snooze strange surprised tambourine terrible tonight
The Flying Machine	**Year 2 High frequency words**
	about after an another back be been brother but by called came can't could did(n't) do don't down first from good got had has have help her here him his home house how if jump(ed) just last lived love made make man must not now off old one out over people pull ran seen so take that their them the these time too two us want(ed) water way were what where who will with would your
	Context words
	aeroplane America auto-pilot captain controls engine flight gasped heavy huge nervous noise passenger pieces roared squashed statue steward straight surprise wondered
Key Trouble	**Year 2 High frequency words**
	about after again an back be but by called came can't did do don't down from girl had has have help her here him his home house jump(ed) just last laugh little love made man more must next not now off old once or our out over push pull put ran saw so some take that them then there these time too took two us want water were what when will with would(n't) your
	Context words
	coloured crashed different downstairs frowned gasped grey minutes mirror nasty naughty photograph piano ready squeezed Squirter tongue upstairs young

Curriculum coverage chart

	Speaking and listening	Reading	Writing
The Blue Eye			
NLS/NC	3a, 3c, 3d, 3e	W1, W7, S4, S5, T2,	T10
Scotland	Level A/B	Level A/B	Level A/B
N. Ireland	Activities: a, f, g Outcomes: a, b, c, d, e	Activities: a, b, e, f Outcomes: b, c, e, f	Outcomes: a, c, f, h, i
Wales	Range: 1, 2, 3 Skills: 1, 2, 3, 4, 5	Range: 1, 2, 4, 5, 6 Skills: 1, 2	Range: 1, 2, 3, 4, 5, 7 Skills: 1, 2, 3, 4, 5, 6, 7, 8
Rescue!			
NLS/NC	1a, 1c, 1d, 8a	W5, W8, S3, T2, T5	T9
Scotland	Level A/B	Level A/B	Level A/B
N. Ireland	Activities: a, c, e, f Outcomes: a, c, d, e, g	Activities: a, b, e, f Outcomes: b, c, e, f	Outcomes: f, g, h, i
Wales	Range: 1, 2, 3, 5 Range: 1, 2, 4, 5, 6	Skills: 1, 2, 3, 4, 5, 6 Skills: 1, 2	Range: 1, 2 Skills: 1, 3, 8
Dutch Adventure			
NLS/NC	2a, 2b	W2, W6, S7, T1, T3	T20
Scotland	Level A/B	Level A/B	Level A/B
N. Ireland	Activities: a, e, g Outcomes: b, c, d	Activities: a, b, c, e Outcomes: b, c, e, f, h, i	Outcomes: b, c, f, h, i
Wales	Range: 1, 2 Skills: 1, 2, 3, 4	Range: 1, 2, 3, 4, 5, 6 Skills: 1, 2, 3	Range: 1, 2, 3, 4, 5, 7 Skills: 1, 2, 3, 4, 5, 6, 7, 8
The Finest in the Land			
NLS/NC	2f, 8b	W3, W9, S1, T1, T16	T11
Scotland	Level A/B	Level A/B	Level A/B
N. Ireland	Activities: b, d, i Outcomes: d, f, g, h, i	Activities: a, b, c, e Outcomes: b, c, e, f, h	Outcomes: a, d, f, g, h, i
Wales	Range: 1, 2, 5 Skills: 1, 2, 4	Range: 1, 2, 4, 5, 6 Skills: 1, 2	Range: 1, 2, 4, 6, 7 Skills: 1, 3, 4, 5, 7, 8
The Flying Machine			
NLS/NC	1b, 1e	W2, W5, S1, S6, T8	T9
Scotland	Level A/B	Level A/B	Level A/B
N. Ireland	Activities: a, g Outcomes: b, c, d, e	Activities: a, b, c, e Outcomes: b, c, e, f	Outcomes: f, h, i
Wales	Range: 1, 2, 3 Skills: 1, 2, 3, 4, 5	Range: 1, 2, 3, 5, 6 Skills: 1, 2	Range: 1, 2 Skills: 1, 3, 8
Key Trouble			
NLS/NC	1e, 2d	W4, W10, S5, T2, T4	T12
Scotland	Level A/B	Level A/B	Level A/B
N. Ireland	Activities: a, f, g Outcomes: a, c, d, e	Activities: a, b, c, e Outcomes: b, c, d, e, f	Outcomes: a, b, c, d, e, f, i
Wales	Range: 1, 2, 3 Skills: 1, 2, 3, 4, 5, 6	Range: 1, 2, 4, 5, 6 Skills: 1, 2, 4	Range: 1, 2, 3, 4, 5, 7 Skills: 1, 3, 4, 5, 6, 7, 8

The Blue Eye

Before reading

● Together, look at the cover. Talk about who is in the aeroplane and on the ground. Ask the children: *Is this a "real life" story or a magic key adventure?*

● Read out the title and ask the children to guess what the blue eye might be. Look through the book to see if they are right.

During reading

● Ask the children to read the story. Praise and encourage as they read. If they get stuck, suggest they try different strategies to work out what a word means, but prompt if they take too long so as not to lose the thread of the story.

Observing Check that the children:

■ are securing phonemic spellings from previous terms: "oo" (took, look); "ar" (marbles, market); "oy" (toys) and "ow" (throw, down) (W1).

Group and independent reading activities

Text level work

Objective To use phonological, contextual, grammatical and graphic knowledge to work out, predict and check the meanings of unfamiliar words and to make sense of what they read (T2).

You will need a piece of A4 paper for each pair of children, and to write these reading clues on the board:

Sound out
Look at letters and punctuation
Is it a thing, description or action?
Read on to find out what it might mean

● In pairs, children cover the illustration on pages 16 and 17 with the A4 paper. Ask one child to read the text on page 16, the other to read page 17. If they get stuck they should help each other by using one or more of the clues on the board.

● Ask the children to remove the paper to see if that helps. The children then read out the passage together.

Do the children understand that they can try different ways to decode the words?

Sentence level work

Objectives To use commas in lists (S4); to write in clear sentences using capital letters and full stops accurately (S5).

You will need sheets of A3 paper for each pair of children to make posters.

- Ask the children to look at pages 12 and 13. Ask: *Can you tell me some of the things in the market?*
- Model writing a poster linking similar items together, e.g. "We sell bananas, melons, tomatoes and nuts." "We sell frying pans, bottles and plates."
- Tell the children they are going to run a market stall for the school fete. Working in pairs, they should make a poster to advertise their goods, using a heading and then listing all the things they will be selling on their stall. They should use proper sentences, linking similar items together, but separating with commas. They can decorate and colour the poster.

Observing Do the children list their items together logically, and do they use "and" without a comma before it?

Word level work

Objective To spell words with common suffixes, e.g. "–ly" (W7).

You will need these word cards: different, busy, strange, narrow, safe, close.

- Write the words "brave" and "beautiful" on the board. Discuss how the use of the word can be changed by adding "–ly", so that it describes how something is done. Give examples.
- Give out the word cards. Each child should write two sentences: first using their word as it is, then another adding "–ly".
- The children then take turns to read out their two sentences to the other children who judge whether they are correct.

Observing Do the children notice that the word "busy" changes its spelling when "–ly" is added?

Speaking and listening activities

Objectives Take turns in speaking (3a); make relevant comments (3c); listen to others' reactions (3d); include relevant detail (3e).

You will need a large blue marble or bead.

● Ask the children to think about what they would like to do to improve the world for everybody. They then take turns to hold the "Blue Eye", each saying what they would do. The other children then vote for who should get it the "Blue Eye" award for the best idea.

Cross-curricular link
◀▶ PSHE: preparing to play an active role as citizens

Writing

Objective To write sustained stories, using their knowledge of story elements: narrative, settings, characterisation, dialogue and the language of story (T10).

You will need an A4 sheet of paper for each child.

● Each child writes at the top of a piece of paper the title of a story called "The Scarlet Scarf".
● They then think of a "good" character and write the name down with a short descriptive term, e.g. "brave", "kind", "caring", "helpful", etc.
● Everyone folds over the top of their paper and passes it to the person to their left.
● The children then write a name and a description of a "bad" character on the paper they have, fold it over and pass it on.
● Next, they write the setting for the story, fold the paper and pass it on.
● Then they think about what the story may be about, write this, fold the paper and pass it on.
● Lastly, each child unfolds his/her paper and then writes a short story around the information on it.

Rescue

Before reading

- Together, look at the cover. Ask the children: *Who is in this story?* Point out that Biff and Wilf were also in *The Blue Eye*. Ask: *What are they doing?*
What can you tell about the story from looking at the cover?
- Read the title and then look through the book, using or pointing out difficult words from the story, e.g. "aeroplane", "gorge", "kidnapped".

During reading

- Ask the children to read the story. Praise and encourage them and if they get stuck, help them to think of ways to work out what a word means. Prompt if necessary. Ask: *Who was Lisa? How did Wilf stop the kidnappers?*

Observing Check that the children:

- read the high frequency words matched to their reading group (W5).
- are using phonological, contextual, grammatical and graphic knowledge to work out, predict and check the meanings of unfamiliar words such as "bounced", "boulder", "landslide" and to make sense of what they are reading (T2).

Group and independent reading activities

Text level work

Objective To read about authors from information on book covers, e.g. other books written, publisher; to become aware of authorship and publication (T5).

You will also need a copy of *The Blue Eye* for each child.

- Ask the children to look at the front and back covers of the two books. What do they find in common? Together, list the similarities on the board: same author, illustrator, characters, publisher, publication date.

- Ask: *Is there anything else which is similar?* (As well as Biff and Wilf, both have the same character Aisha and the same villains. You might want to point out that on page 30 of *The Blue Eye* you can see the villain peering through the window!).
- Each child should write down two things they can tell from the cover which are common to the two books.

Observing Can the children find the publication date in the imprint information?

Sentence level work

Objective To use standard forms of verbs in speaking and writing and to use the past tense consistently for narration (S3).

You will need these word cards: are, come, go, fly, has, hear, hold, is, run, take.

- Give each pair of children a card. Ask one of the children to use that word in a sentence correctly, e.g. "I hear someone playing a drum". The other child puts the sentence into the past tense, using reported speech, e.g. "Abdul said that he heard someone playing a drum." The children then pass their card to the next pair and receive another.

Observing Do the children understand that reported speech is always in the past tense?

Word level work

Objective To spell common irregular words (W8).

You will need sets of the following word cards: after, another, first, many, one, put, their, there, water, were, would, your.

- With the cards in a pile face down, the children sit around a table. Each child takes two cards. The children take it in turns to read out one word and the other children try to write each word on a piece of paper with their name on it. The children then take turns to read the second words, while the other children write the words. The children swap papers and mark the spelling, checking against the cards.

Observing Have the children learned these irregular words or are they trying to spell them phonetically?

Speaking and listening activities

Objectives Speak with clear diction and appropriate intonation (1a); organize what they say (1c); focus on the main point(s) (1d); tell stories (8a).

- Choose a child in the group to be Lisa while the other children ask her these questions: How did you feel when you were kidnapped?
  How did you feel when you saw that Princess Asia had come to rescue you?
  What did you think of Biff and Wilf?
  How were you rescued?
  What happened then?
- The group should then check to see if "Lisa" was correct in her account of the rescue.

Writing

Objective Through shared and guided writing to apply phonological, graphic knowledge and sight vocabulary to spell words accurately (T9).

- Write the first two sentences from page 19 on the board. Talk about which words are spelled according to how they sound, e.g. "steep" and which are not, e.g. "was", "rough".
- Dictate the following ten words for the children to write down: bolted, bones, creep, goose, socks, sorry, toad, tough, window, jumped.
- Write the answers above the similar words that are on the board for the children to check against. Did the children spell all ten words correctly?

Dutch Adventure

Before reading

- Together, look at the cover. Ask the children: *Where do you think the children might be? Why do you think this?* Read the title and praise the children who guessed correctly. Ask: *What is on the back of the cart? Can you guess what the story might be about?*
- Go through the book using unfamiliar words such as "dyke", "bicycle" and "diamonds", so that they will be known when the children come to read them.

During reading

- Ask the children to read the story. Praise and encourage them while they read. Prompt where necessary but encourage them to use the pictures to help them. Ask: *Why did the man on the bicycle want his own cheese back? Did Hans get some money after all?*

Observing Check that the children:

- are aware that "they" and "key" have the same spelling pattern but sound different (W6)
- use their word-level skills to work out difficult words (T1).

Group and independent reading activities

Text level work

Objective To notice the difference between spoken and written forms through re-telling known stories; compare oral versions with the written text (T3).

You will need a miniature Edam cheese, a whistle or drum.

- In a circle, ask the children to pass round the cheese. When you blow the whistle or bang the drum, call out one of the characters from the story, including the thief. The child who is holding the cheese tells the story from the character's point of view. Tell the children they can describe feelings and emotions but they must stick to the events in the story.
- When everyone has had a turn the children check their books to see whether their oral versions were correct.

Observing Do the children use their own words to get into character?

Sentence level work

Objectives To compare a variety of forms of questions from texts, e.g. asking for help (S7).

You will need these word cards: Dad, Biff, Chip, Trudy, Hans, the thief.

- Tell the children to look through the story, noting where people ask or offer help. Give each child a character card. Encourage the children to ask for help, trying to use different words from those that were used in the book, and from each other, e.g. "Please can…"; "Will you…"; "Could you…"; "Can you…"; "Could you possibly…"; "I wonder whether you could…"; "May we…", etc.

Observing Are the children asking the questions with the correct intonation?

Word level work

Objective To reinforce work on discriminating syllables in reading and spelling from previous term: splitting familiar oral and written compound words into component parts (W2).

You will need cards with simple words on them to make into compound words, e.g. air, bag, ball, bed, craft, hand, man, post, room, tea.

- Ask the children if they can find some compound words in the story (where a new word is made up of two or more other words). Can they find base/ball, wind/mill, bed/room?
- Give out the word cards to the group and see how many compound words they can list. Ask the children to read out their new words.

Observing Are the children splitting the words into the correct number of syllables when they read them out?

Speaking and listening activities

Objectives Sustain concentration (2a); remember specific points that interest them (2b).

- Ask the children, in pairs, to look through the book, noting how olden-day Holland differs from where they live today. Then choose some of the pairs to tell the others what they noticed, e.g. the land is very flat, there are dykes and there are lots of windmills; the women wear ornate, curly hats and embroidered dresses with aprons, and the people wear clogs; the houses in the village have pointed roofs, gaily painted shutters and decorations on the eaves.

Cross-curricular link

◀▶ Geography: where in the world is Barnaby Bear?

Writing

Objective To write non-fiction texts, using texts read as models for own writing, e.g. use of headings, sub-headings, captions (T20).

You may need reference books on cheese and you will need to write the following questions on the board:

1. What is cheese made from?
2. What does it look like?
3. What does it taste like?
4. What different kinds of cheese are there?
5. What can you make with cheese?
6. Which places sell cheese?

- Discuss the questions above about cheese.
- Tell the children they are going to make a book about cheese to give to the Reception or Year 1 class. Give each child a sentence number. On a separate piece of paper under their sentence heading the child writes about his or her question, accompanying the piece with a labeled drawing. Encourage the children to use reference books to help them.
- The six pages can be stapled to make a booklet to give to the Reception or Year 1 class to read.

The Finest in the Land

Before reading

- Together, look at the cover. Ask the children: *What are the children doing? Can you name the musical instruments?* Which children are playing the same instruments?
- Read the title and ask the children to try to guess what it is about. Look through the book to see if they are right.

During reading

- Ask the children to read the story. Praise and encourage them if they get stuck, prompting where necessary. Encourage them to use phonological and graphemic skills as well as illustrations to help with unusual words such as "kazoo" and "mixture". Ask: *Why did Hugh's friends pretend to be entertainers? Do you think the king will be angry with Edith and Hugh when he wakes up?*

Observing Check that the children:

- can discriminate, spell and read the phonemes "ear" ("hear") and "ea" ("ready") (W3)
- are applying their word-level skills (T1).

Group and independent reading activities

Text level work

Objective To scan a text to find specific sections, e.g. key words or phrases (T16).

You will need a dictionary for each pair of children, and three Post-it notes for each dictionary to mark pages.

- Ask the children, in pairs, to go through the storybook listing all the words they can find which have to do with entertaining: band, entertain(ers), guitar, instruments, juggler, kazoo, musicians, play, practise, recorder, sing(ing), song, stilts, tambourine, tune.
- Ask the children to look up definitions in their dictionary for three of the words, marking the pages with a Post-it note. Choose some children to read them out.

Observing Are the children using their alphabetic skills to find the words in the dictionary?

Sentence level work

Objective   To read text aloud with intonation and expression appropriate to the grammar and punctuation (S1).

● Choose four children to read pages 24, 25 and 26 of the story: a narrator, the Duke, John and Wilma. They should be given time to read the text carefully and practise using an appropriate voice, first on their own, then together, reading only the words of their own character. The children then read the passage to the class putting in as much expression as they can: the Duke booming, John begging, Wilma whispering.

Observing   Did the children read the descriptions of their characters' voices carefully before they read aloud, e.g. shouted, begged, whispered?

Word level work

Objective   New words from reading linked to particular topics, to build individual collections of personal interest or significant words (W9).

● Ask: *Who can play a musical instrument? What is it?* Write the instruments that the children play on the board, then ask if any members of their families play different ones and add those. What other instruments do they know? Help them by contributing to the collection. You could add some unusual ones such as the trombone, ukulele, French horn, zither, mbira (African finger drum).
● Ask the children to put the instrument words into alphabetical order, choose one instrument to draw, and label its various parts.

Observing   Can the children alphabetise beyond the first letter, e.g. triangle, trumpet?

Speaking and listening activities

Objectives   Identify and respond to sound patterns in language (2f); read aloud and recite (8b).

You will need to write this silly rhyme on the board (or make up one using the theme of the book):

We are the finest in the land,
In all the land, the finest band.
We'll sing our songs as best we can,
Give us a hand, we'll take the stand.

- Give the children some time to work out a way of performing the rhyme. They could either take turns to say the lines separately, or they could chant them together. Alternatively, they could make up a tune and sing it.
- Ask the group to perform it for the rest of the class.

Cross-curricular link
◀▶ Music: feel the pulse: exploring pulse and rhythm

Writing

Objective   To write tongue-twisters or alliterative sentences; select words with care, re-reading and listening to their effect. (T11).

- Explain what a tongue-twister is and give an example, e.g. "Round and round the rugged rock the ragged rascal ran"; "She sells seashells on the seashore".
- Tell the children that the sleeping mixture in the story still isn't working and they are going to have to help the children in the story to entertain the Duke. They must invent tongue-twisters to make him laugh.
- Together, think of some simple "s" and "sh" words which could be used to make sentences, e.g. sea, sinking, shoddy, ship, should, slipping, slithery, sloppy, slowly, stop, sharp, skinny, smelly, small.
- The children attempt to write their own tongue-twister, using the words discussed or others they can think of, and take turns to read it out.

The Flying Machine

Before reading

- Together, look at the cover. Ask the children: *What are Nadim and Anneena running away from?*
- Read the title. Ask: *Do you think the story is set in the present or the past?*
- Look through the book at the pictures and talk about the settings (the plane, Biff's room, the open country). Ask: *Has anyone ever been on an aeroplane? Was it fun?*

During reading

- Ask the children to read the story. Encourage them to respond to words like "shouted", "gasped", "yelled", and to read with expression, praising them for their efforts.

Observing   Check that the children:

- can discriminate syllables in their reading, e.g. home, air/port, ho/li/day, A/me/ri/ca (W2)
- read text aloud with intonation and expression appropriate to the grammar and punctuation (S1).

Group and independent reading activities

Text level work

Objective   To discuss meanings of words and phrases that create humour, and sound effects in poetry, e.g. nonsense poems, tongue-twisters, riddles (T8).

- Ask the children: *What did Harold think Nadim said when he said, "We've not seen an aeroplane like this before"?* (hairy plane). Talk about ways in which writers can use language to make a story funny, e.g. by using assonance or alliteration, riddles, puns, or tongue twisters.
- In pairs, ask the children to brainstorm sound words for the runaway plane. They need not be real words. Write their contributions on the board.

- Ask the children to use the words, and others they think of, to make up nonsense phrases or sentences about the flying machine. Put them together to make a poem, e.g.

Bump, bump, rumpety trump,
Flip, flap, flop.
Vroom, shroom, garoomity goom
Crish, crash, snap!

- Let the children read out the poem together, stressing the sounds.

Observing Do the children recognise that words with the same letters usually sound alike, e.g. "fl" in "flip, flap, flop" or "oo" in "vroom, shroom"?

Sentence level work

Objective To turn statements into questions, learning a range of "wh" words typically used to open questions: what, where, when, who, and to add question marks (S6).

You will need these word cards: Who? What? Where? When?

- Write the following on the board:

Nadim and Anneena
a strange-looking car
America
back in time.

- Ask the children to look at pages 8 and 9 of the story.
- Give out one question card to a child. The child asks a relevant question, using the text, and chooses someone to select an answer from the board. Give out another question card to a different child for them to think of a "who", "what", "where" or "when" question to ask from the story.
- Each child could then write four questions about the story starting with each question word.

Observing Have the children remembered to put a question mark at the end of each sentence?

Word level work

Objective To read on sight high frequency words likely to occur in graded texts matched to the abilities of reading groups (W5).

You will need blank cards or small card-sized pieces of paper for the children to write on.

- Write the following words on the board: always, everyone, idea, heavy, learn, middle, mother, noise, please, through.
- Ask the children to write these words on their cards in their very best writing, giving them each three words to write. Collect the cards and shuffle them. Children come up in turn, pick a card and read it.

Observing Are the children using graphic and phonemic strategies to decode the words?

Speaking and listening activities

Objectives Choose words with precision (1b); include relevant detail (1e).

- Each child thinks of something they would like to invent, what they would use to make it, and how it would work. They then describe their invention to others.
- The children could attempt to make their invention using reclaimed materials such as cotton reels and rubber bands.

Cross-curricular link
◀▶ Design and Technology: winding up

Writing

Objective Through shared and guided writing to apply phonological, graphic knowledge and sight vocabulary to spell words accurately (T9).

You will need a tray with the following on it: a bookmark, facecloth, hairbrush, handbag, lipstick, matchbox, postcard, teaspoon.

- Talk about compound words, putting some examples on the board, e.g. "airport", "toothpick", "postman".
- Tell the children that your friend, like Nadim, has just come back from holiday, and has brought you some gifts. You know that all the gifts are one word made up of two but you need their help to spell them to write a thank you letter.
- Hold each "gift" up, saying what it is as you do so. Ask them to write down the word for each object.
- Write the spellings on the board and ask the children to swap papers and mark them. Did anyone spell them all correctly?

Observing Do the children understand what compound words are?
Do they use their knowledge of vowel phonemes to write the words, e.g. "ea" as in "teaspoon"?

Key Trouble

Before reading

You will need some old black and white photographs.

- Show the children some old photographs, explaining that photographs and films used to be black and white. Together, look at the book cover. Ask the children: *Who is going on this magic key adventure? Does he look pleased? Why do you think the background (the vortex) is black and white?*
- Read the title and look through the book at the pictures. Ask: *Have you ever seen a black and white film on television?*

During reading

- Ask the children to read the story. Praise and encourage them while they read, helping them to use reading strategies if necessary.
- Ask: *Do you think Mum and Dad were pleased with Gran? Was the magic key right to punish Kipper?*

Observing Check that the children:

- can read high frequency words (W4)
- are using a variety of strategies to work out unfamiliar words (T2).

Group and independent reading activities

Text level work

Objective To compare books by same author: settings, characters, themes; to evaluate and form preferences, giving reasons (T4).

You will need a copy of each of the Stage 9 More Stories A storybooks placed in a box with a cover.

- Ask for a volunteer to talk about *Key Trouble*. Give the child a copy of the book and ask him/her to tell you who it's by, who the main character is, where it is set and to say very briefly what it is about.
- Ask another volunteer to come up and, without looking, pick a book from the box. He/she should compare the book with *Key Trouble*, talking about the author, characters, setting, and a sentence to say how the story is similar or different.
- Do this with two more books, then ask some of the children to tell you which book they preferred and why.

Are the children able to justify their preferences with good reasons?

Sentence level work

Objective To write in clear sentences using capital letters and full stops accurately (S5).

- Look at pages 4 and 5 of the story. Ask: *Can you tell which is Gran in the pictures? What is she wearing in each picture? How is her hair different?*
- Ask the children to write three sentences about Gran as a little girl, as a young mother when Mum was little, and what she is like now.

Observing Have the children used capital letters for "Mum" and "Gran", as well as the start of the sentences?

Word level work

Objective To use synonyms and other alternative words/phrases that express same or similar meanings; to collect, discuss similarities and shades of meaning and use to extend and enhance writing (W10).

- Point out to the children that the characters in the stories often say "Brilliant". Can they think of other words to say the same thing? (Accept slang expressions such as "cool" and "wicked", as well as, e.g. "great", "super", "okay".)
- Ask each child to make up four sentences using the following four words: old, laughed, tiny and funny.
- When they have written them down ask them to show their sentences to a partner. Can the partner think of another word that means the same thing? Alternatives for each word include: old (aged, ancient, elderly); laughed (giggled, sniggered, joked); tiny (little, small, petty, minute) and funny (odd, strange, silly, laughable).
- Talk about the best choice for the sentence.

Observing Is the children's vocabulary wide enough to distinguish shades of meaning in the alternatives?

Speaking and listening activities

Objectives   Include relevant detail (1e); listen to others' reactions (2d).

● The children should close their eyes for a few minutes and think of the world around them and all the colours in it. Then they open their eyes and take turns to describe the three things they would miss most if the world was in black and white. The children vote on which were the best three things described. Does everyone agree? If not, why not?

Writing

Objective   To write simple evaluations of books read and discussed giving reasons (T12).

You will need photocopies of a review sheet, one for each child, e.g.

Name:
The title is…
The story is by…
The main characters are…
I liked the part when….
I think you will like this book because…

● Ask the children to write a review of *Key Trouble* using the key headings and phrases.

Oxford Reading Tree resources at this level

There is a range of material available at a similar level to these stories which can be used for consolidation or extension.

Stage 9

Teacher support
- Teacher's Handbook
- Guided Reading Cards for Stage 9 Stories
- Take-Home Card for each story
- BBC Storytapes + Teacher's Activity Book
- Stage 9 Workbooks 4–6
- Woodpeckers Photocopy Masters
- Group Activity Sheets Book 3 Stages 6–9
- ORT Games Stages 6–9

Further reading
- Robins (for extended reading practice)
- Jackdaws Anthologies
- Woodpeckers: Anthologies 8–10
- Citizenship Stories
- Fireflies Non-Fiction
- ORT True Stories (narrative non-fiction)
- Fact Finders Unit F
- Conkers and More Conkers Poetry
- Jackdaws and More Jackdaws Poetry

Electronic
- Clip Art
- Stage 8 and 9 Talking Stories
- ORT Online www.OxfordReadingTree.com
- Floppy and Friends

OXFORD
UNIVERSITY PRESS

Great Clarendon Street, Oxford OX2 6DP

Oxford University Press is a department of the University of Oxford. It furthers the University's objective of excellence in research, scholarship, and education by publishing worldwide in

Oxford New York

Auckland Cape Town Dar es Salaam Hong Kong Karachi Kuala Lumpur Madrid Melbourne Mexico City Nairobi New Delhi Shanghai Taipei Toronto

With offices in

Argentina Austria Brazil Chile Czech Republic France Greece Guatemala Hungary Italy Japan Poland Portugal Singapore South Korea Switzerland Thailand Turkey Ukraine Vietnam

Oxford is a registered trade mark of Oxford University Press in the UK and in certain other countries

© Oxford University Press 2003

The moral rights of the author have been asserted

Database right Oxford University Press (maker)

First published 2003

British Library Cataloguing in Publication Data

Data available

Cover illustrations Alex Brychta

Teacher's Notes: ISBN-13   978-0-19-845293-5
ISBN-10 0-19-845293-4

10 9 8 7

Page make-up by IFA Design Ltd, Plymouth, Devon

Printed in China by Imago